E.W. KENYON
Author

Published by

KENYON'S GOSPEL PUBLISHING SOCIETY

ISBN# 1-57770-012-0

TABLE OF CONTENTS

FIRST WORDS

This is a challenging study of a vital issue that touches the heart of our restless age.

Faith's landmarks are nearly all erased.

We are groping for the path that will lead us to the Light.

THE APPROACH

O, I have never been able to accept the Bible as a Revelation."

"Why?"

"Because it is a miracle book. It begins with miracles. It sponsors miracles. Every one of the healing characters was a miracle worker, until finally we come to Jesus.

"I recognize him as the most outstanding product of the human family. But I cannot accept him as being conceived independent of natural generation.

"I cannot understand a Resurrection. They are both contrary to human experience and reasoning.

"There are no such things as miracles."

"But don't you believe that there is a God?"

"I believe there is some force that we cannot understand, that is out of the reach of human knowledge; but as for a personal God, I have no evidence.

"I have given forty years to scientific investigation in Physics, Chemistry, and Biology, but I cannot find God."

"Would you like to believe there is a God if it could be proven that He exists and is an intelligent God of love?"

"Yes, I would, but there is no way to find Him. I have sought through every avenue of human investigation, and He is not there."

"If I should tell you, doctor, that there was a way of finding Him, would it seem credible to you? But first, let me show you why you take the mental attitude that you do.

"You know that all the knowledge that we have today in the Mechanical, Chemical, Metallurgical, and Scientific fields has come from one source."

Here the doctor looked very much interested. His keen, intelligent eyes widened. "Yes, I recognize that," he said, "All this knowledge comes from our Five Senses. I have often thought of it. These Five Senses—Hearing, Smelling, Tasting, Feeling, and Seeing—are the doors into the brain."

"Yes, doctor, but we cannot belittle these servants. They have given to the world knowledge that seems almost incredible.

"When you were a boy, the electric car was just coming in. Men were just writing about steam wagons. Electricity was almost unknown as we view it today.

"You have lived through the greatest inventive, creative age of human history. All the knowledge that has been gained these last seventy years has been gained through these Five Senses.

"All the knowledge that is taught in the academies, schools, and universities, is what we are going to call Sense Knowledge."

The doctor spoke again. This time his voice was low and vibrant with feeling. "There are limitations to this Sense Knowledge as you call it, serious limitations."

The other answered him. "We cannot know God through the Senses. Had we been able to find Him, things would have been different.

"Neither can we know the Reason for Creation, nor the Reason for man. We cannot find in all our searchings the source of Light, of Life, of Motion, of Gravitation, and a hundred other things before which the world stands baffled and confused.

"You see, doctor, Sense Knowledge has been unable to explain the apparent design in Creation, where every need of this Scientific and Mechanical age is being met in the metals, chemicals, vegetables, and in the air and water. This fact alone proves that someone planned it. Someone knew the age of Mechanics and Chemistry was coming and prepared for it."

The doctor merely assented. His friend said, "You have noted, then, the limitations. Now I would like to suggest to you the solution of this problem.

"I wish to show you the bridge that crosses the chasm that Sense Knowledge faces.

"You know whenever man has reached the limit of Sense Knowledge, he at once turns philosopher or guesser."

The doctor smiled and said, "Most of our scientific books are beautiful guesses. I know of no guesser in the class with Darwin."

Then his face grew serious and he said, "What is this solution?"

His friend answered, "It is another kind of Knowledge. It is Revelation Knowledge, if we may so call it. For argument's sake let us assume, for a moment, that there is a God and that this wonderful earth of ours was designed and created by this God.

"One more assumption—man comes on the scene. Man is the reason for this earth. God created this earth for His man, who was coming.

"That would give us the reason for creation and the reason for man, and it would suggest the nature of man, that man would be a spirit in the same class with the God who created him to be His companion.

"Then it would be the most natural thing in the world if God should wish to communicate with this man, and if He did communicate with him, He would need to come to man's level. It would have to be a communication that the Senses could understand. It would be in the realm of Sense Knowledge.

"It would need to be written through men whom He controlled, men who yielded themselves to His sway and wrote as He moved them."

The doctor looked up and said, "That's credible, but that's a miracle."

"But you see, doctor, spiritual things are just as real as material things and there are spiritual realities as well as material realities.

"God is a spirit. Man is a spirit. He lives in a body. He has a soul composed of intellect and reasoning faculties.

"The thing we call sub-conscious mind is nothing else than his spirit, the real man. It would be the most normal thing that God should communicate with this man, and man should be able to communicate with Him.

"So you see that the book we call the Bible is a reasonable thing, a natural thing, and a thing that man actually demands.

"You know that all men are religious. This is spirit hunger for God. Man is really God-hungry. This is because he was created to be the companion of God. Man is God-lonesome. You will admit that you are a searcher after God."

The doctor's fine, beautiful head was bent. He was leaning on his hands. He did not answer. There was silence for a few moments; then he said, "I wish I knew that this were true. If this Bible is a Revelation, it would solve the human problem."

They sat in silence again, then the doctor, speaking more to himself than to his companion said, "That book tells us of the Reason for Creation, its Origin, the source of Life and Light.

"I can see now, how Revelation Knowledge is necessary to Sense Knowledge. They should never be separated one from the other."

This conversation took place in the lobby of a hotel.

It will illustrate the mental attitude of the leading minds of the scholastic world.

This will introduce you to the subject of this little book; now read and live!

Chapter One

THE ACHIEVEMENTS AND LIMITATIONS
OF SENSE KNOWLEDGE

EW of us have realized that the great body of knowledge that has been accumulated through the ages has come to us through the Five Senses. The human body has really been the laboratory for the testing and investigation of all human activities.

Every step in the fields of Chemistry, Mechanics, Metallurgy, Surgery, Mental Sciences, and the Arts, has come from this one common source.

The Five Senses, the humbled, abused Senses, are the five servants that have been conveying knowledge of every sort and kind to the brain for it to classify, number, and file away for future use.

It is said that Mr. Edison experimented more than three thousand times with the incandescent lamp before he arrived.

Each mechanical invention, the Radio, the Adding Machine, the Typewriter, has gone through a series of experimentations and developments since its first conception.

This will cause you to see the painstaking, patient research work that men have done in order to give us what we have today in the Mechanical, Scientific, and Chemical world. We would like to pay our tribute to this patient, hard working body of men in the field of scientific research, who have given us the benefits of all their labor in their respective fields.

The Five Senses—Sight, Feeling, Hearing, Tasting, and

Smelling—are the parents of all this knowledge.

They are not always reliable.

The Senses may become impaired by accident, carelessness, overwork, or dissipation, so that they are not to be depended upon. They are not absolutely true.

Their findings are continually being revised.

Their limitations are known and reckoned upon.

Yet what ministers they have been.

We would not, for one moment, criticize them.

We know where their frontiers are located.

They cannot know the beginning of things.

They can only speculate when they arrive at the last frontier of experimentation.

They know nothing of:

> The Reason for Creation
> The Reason and Origin of Man
> The Origin of Life
> The Origin of Motion
> The Origin of Matter
> The Origin of Force

Standing on the edge of this last frontier of their limitations, the mind is unsatisfied.

It craves knowledge, and so, unconsciously, it becomes speculative. It begins to evolve theories.

Reason has no data, no absolute facts on which it can build. It can only dream now and theorize.

Dr. Darwin stood out on the last frontier of human experimentation. He had reached the very limit.

The Darwinian theory of Evolution was born out of his lack of knowledge of the Reason for Creation, the Origin of

Matter, of Light, of Motion, of Gravitation.

He was unwilling to accept Revelation Knowledge that, at this point of his extremity, would have helped him bridge the chasm and put his feet upon solid ground.

His Sense Knowledge could not find God, so he could not believe in God.

Sense Knowledge can see the handiwork of God, can see the design in Creation, but it cannot find the Designer; it is often unwilling to admit that there is a Designer, because it cannot find Him.

He could not find life in the plant that he dissected, yet he admitted there was life.

He could not see thought, yet he believed in it.

He could not see the brain function, yet he knew that it did.

There seems to be a little inconsistency in the man who refuses to admit anything beyond the range of Sense Knowledge.

The telescope of Sense Knowledge marks his horizon.

There Darwin began to guess and theorize, and he gave to us the great master guess: Evolution.

He had reached the place where Revelation Knowledge was imperative.

He refused that and stepped out into the darkness of Sense Knowledge.

He bridged impassable chasms, one after another with a guess.

The Revelation of God was the missing link that he needed.

Not believing in God, he had to find the solution of a

universe.

Revelation would have supplemented his limited knowledge and he would have stood shoulder to shoulder with Lord Kelvin and the other great scientists of his day who believed in God.

But he repudiated Revelation, forgetting that he had reached the unknowable in Creation in a hundred places.

If our modern educators could realize the limitations of Sense Knowledge and know that the Bible holds the key to their quest, they would have the real conclusion of Creation's story.

Chapter Two

THE REVELATION

HE BIBLE stands alone among the books of the world.

Its outstanding characteristic, which differentiates it from every other book, is that it is a Revelation from God to man.

It demands man's obedience; claims man as its subject.

It does not profess to be a scientific treatise, but it is the mother of all sciences.

It has given birth to our Educational Systems, to our Philanthropic enterprises, our Mechanical, Chemical, and Biological discoveries.

No nation ever needed a patent or a copyright law until this Revelation Book had been given to it.

Germany never awakened in Chemistry or Mechanics until the Bible had been put into her mother tongue.

The same thing was true in England.

This Revelation has come to us on the level of Sense Knowledge, in language we can understand.

It is a Revelation of the Reason for Creation.

It is a Revelation of the Way of Creation, how it actually came into being by faith, and that the Creator is a Faith God.

This is perfectly in harmony with all the facts that Sense Knowledge has gathered.

It is the man of faith who creates things in the Mechanical, Architectural, and Industrial world.

Faith is the creative force in man.

14

Faith is the creative force in the Creator.

God simply said, "Let there be."

The Bible is a Revelation of the Reason for man, the nature of man, and the destiny of man.

It is a Revelation of the source of Life.

It is a Revelation of sin and its origin and of man's Redemption from its dominion and authority.

It is a Revelation of the why of the Jewish nation.

It is a Revelation of the most outstanding character of human history, the Man of Galilee, proved to be the Son of God by His Resurrection from the dead.

It is a Revelation of a perfect Redemption on legal grounds.

It is a Revelation of a New Creation created in Christ Jesus.

It is a Revelation of the family of God, of man's place in the heart dream of the Creator.

It is a Revelation of the cause of sin, suffering, and death, and of their final destruction.

It is a Revelation of a New Heaven and a New Earth and man's eternity with God in perfect bliss.

This Revelation is necessary to Sense Knowledge.

It crowns Sense Knowledge.

It shows how the human intellect, that has been debauched by sin and generations of wrong thinking, can come into perfect fellowship with the Creator God.

It is a Revelation of God as a Father, and of this Father God as a God of Love.

The denial and repudiation of Revelation Knowledge has been the darkest blot upon the modern scholastic mind which owes its very growth and development to this Revelation.

Chapter Three

SOME SENSE KNOWLEDGE FACTS

O ONE ever saw an atom; yet the scientific world profoundly believes in them.

No one ever saw an electron and yet men spend years searching for them.

The silent pictures thrown upon the screen mean nothing to the blind.

The noisy radio means nothing to the deaf.

The deeply spiritual things mean nothing to the man of Sense Knowledge, who has dwarfed his spirit nature, kept it in bondage, undeveloped, like a child chained in a garret without book or instructor.

Is it any wonder that the Psalmist cried, "Bring my soul out of prison, and I will praise thee"?

Reason holds the same relation to the spirit that the body does to Reason.

When the body rules reason, chaos and calamity are certain.

It is also true that when reason rules your spirit, calamity is inevitable.

Someone says, "But how can I develop my spirit?"

Spirit development comes through fellowship with the Father-God, through His Revelation.

The mind becomes Renewed until it can know and understand the Father's will in this Revelation.

The heart, by feeding upon this Revelation, comes into the closest fellowship with the Father; its life becomes keyed to the pitch of His will.

Just as Sense Knowledge is developed by reading Sense

Knowledge literature, so the spirit grows by reading and meditating in the Revelation that was designed to be its food, for "Man shall not live by bread alone, but by every Word that proceedeth out of the mouth of God."

We have accepted His Revelation, and we know that He is a person.

We know that He can reveal Himself to our spirits so that we are as sure of spiritual realities as we are of the realities of the Senses.

We know that He is the Creator, the Sustainer, and Ruler of this universe.

We know that He is a spirit, and we know that man is in His class of spirit being, and can become a partaker of His nature.

We know that man can contact Him; that he can speak with Him, and that God hears him.

We know that God finds His highest Joy in fellowship with man, and man reaches his highest development in fellowship with God.

We know that God is a faith God, and that He brought the universe into being by the Word of Faith. This universe was to be the home of His man.

He said, "Let there be light," and there was light.

He said, "Let there be an earth," and the earth came into being.

Then He said, "Let there be vegetation," and it came.

"Let there be animal life," and it came.

"Let us make man."

He also said, "Let there be lights in the firmament of heaven to give light upon the earth," and the sun and moon and stars and the constellations leaped into being fresh from the womb of the faith of God.

He is not only a faith God, but He is a Love God.

He is Love.

He has faith.

You can understand why natural faith that comes from man's spirit has been in the creators and the inventors of the ages.

All great achievements of man have been faith achievements.

The great achievements of God are faith achievements.

The thing that calls the achievements into being is love.

Now you can understand why God demands faith from your spirit in His Word, because God cannot communicate with you through the Senses.

He can communicate with your spirit.

Faith is not the product of the Senses, it is the product of your spirit.

Consequently He demands faith of you, not of your reason, but of your spirit.

When He said, "Thou shalt love the Lord thy God with all thy heart and soul and mind," He was talking to man's spirit, for man's reasoning faculties cannot love.

Man cannot love a woman or a man through his reason.

It is your spirit that loves.

We talk about the heart loving. The heart is just a figurative term for the spirit.

So Faith is a spirit product and your spirit is the real you.

The spirit in you should have the dominance over your reasoning faculties, just as your reasoning faculties have the dominance over your body.

Chapter Four

"EXPERIENCE IS THE BEST TEACHER"

 HIS is the slogan of Sense Knowledge.

"Seeing is believing" is another favorite.

Revelation or Faith Knowledge seems unbelievable and impossible to the man who has only Sense Knowledge.

If I did not know that man was a spirit and created to be the companion of God, I would be hopeless; but I know that his spirit is God hungry, and whether he has ever been able to interpret the longing and continual yearning in his being after something that seems unattainable or not, makes no difference.

I know that yearning is after God.

It may lead him to the dance hall.

It may lead him to drink.

It may lead him to all kinds of excesses which have never answered the cry of his being.

But if the right message is given to man, his spirit will come to the place of ascendancy and will compel his reasoning faculties to listen.

We have failed to recognize this tremendous fact. There are two kinds of Knowledge.

One kind of Knowledge has to do with the spirit of man and the other has to do with his senses.

We have not realized that spirit hunger is as real as physical or mental hunger.

We haven't realized that the Bible or Revelation Knowledge was designed by the Author primarily to answer this

19

spirit cry and to satisfy the hunger of the spirit.

Jesus knew it for He said, "Man shall not live by bread alone, but by every Word that proceedeth out of the mouth of God."

Jesus came not only to minister to man's body, but to minister to his spirit.

The miracles that Jesus performed in the Sense Realm were to prove to men of the Sense Realm that He was God.

Revelation or Faith Knowledge is in the realm above Sense Knowledge.

It is hard for Sense Knowledge folks to grasp it.

By experience they have learned much, and it is hard to have to come to them now with Grace.

All Sense Knowledge comes by works.

Grace Knowledge comes by faith.

It is so revolutionary that it is hard for them to grasp it.

Sense Knowledge has all come by hard work, close application and sacrifice.

The man that has climbed to the top in the business world, in the professional world or in the inventive, creative world, knows that every step of his progress has been by self denial and hard work.

Now I come to him with something far superior to anything he has ever known in the Sense Realm. I tell him it is all of grace, on the ground of Faith.

He is not a trifler; he is an honest man.

He looks at me in amazement and says, "It can't be. If I could acquire this spiritual knowledge through the same channel of hard work, I could accept it, but you are asking me to accept by faith something that I cannot reason out.

"I can't understand it. You tell me that Jesus was an Incarnation; that God was manifest in the flesh.

"That is contrary to anything I have ever known.

"You tell me that God made Christ to be sin with my sin; that He suffered in my stead. I can't grasp it.

"There is no point of contact with the Senses.

"You tell me that He arose from the dead. That is entirely outside of the field of human experience or of Sense Knowledge.

"You are asking me to believe a thing that gives Sense Knowledge no basis upon which to build.

"I believe in things I can see. I can hear, I can feel, I can taste or smell. I believe in material things, because I can feel them and see them. But I cannot believe in God because I cannot see Him. He does not speak to me.

"You ask me to believe in miracles. Miracles are outside of the realm of Sense Knowledge.

Sense Knowledge says that faith cannot produce miracles like healing diseases and setting bones.

It is unreasonable.

Then I ask my Sense Knowledge friend if he can see love.

He must acknowledge that he cannot.

He can see the effect of love, but he cannot see love.

Love is of the spirit.

Love does not belong to the Reason Realm.

Love did not come through the avenues of the Senses.

Love is not produced by feeling, by hearing, by seeing. (I am talking about divine Love. What we ofttime call physical love or Sense Knowledge love is nothing but creative passion. We are dealing now with spirit things.)

Love is of your spirit.

You cannot see hatred.

You cannot feel it, nor hear it.

Yet it is one of the most powerful forces in the world.

You cannot see, nor hear, nor feel thought, but you know it is a reality.

You cannot see the imagination, yet it can take the pictures of Sense Knowledge and throw them upon a canvas, or can translate them into the most beautiful harmony.

You cannot see some of what we call natural phenomena.

You cannot see the wind, but you can see the effect of it.

You cannot see gravitation. You can feel the effect of it.

You cannot see conscience, the voice of your spirit, but you can feel the effect of it.

You see there are very few of the greater things of life that the Senses register.

They register the effect but they cannot grasp the fact, the reality.

God is a spirit. Man is a spirit.

They belong to the same class of being.

Man's spirit is the real man.

His Senses are but the servants of this real man.

His reasoning faculties are servants of this real man, the spirit.

The scripture calls it, "The inward man of the heart."

My physical body contacts physical things.

My mind contacts thoughts.

My spirit can contact God.

Reason is the light that is shed by the oil of the Senses.

Conscience is the voice of the spirit.

Science is but arranged facts that the Senses have discovered.

Science has become the god of the scholastic world.

Ages ago the Senses built gods of wood, and of stone, and of gold, because they were God hungry.

Man is still God hungry and now instead of building idols out of wood, and stone, and metal, he builds them out of Sense Knowledge.

He is worshipping still the work of his hands.

He can't help it.

His Science does not explain the reason for Creation, nor the Reason for man, and Science cannot discover spirit, nor can it find life.

He can see the effect of the spirit, the effect of life.

Science cannot answer the why of man's being nor where he is going.

Science cannot answer this age-long hunger after God, nor of man's unconscious faith in a life beyond the grave.

Science, as we know it today, is the blind child of the Senses.

Chapter Five

THE LIMITS OF SENSE KNOWLEDGE

SENSE Knowledge is limited to what the Senses are capable of assimilating.

If they are impaired by blindness, or deafness, or the loss of the sense of taste, or smell, the experimenter is handicapped.

In the scientific world, man's body has become a laboratory, his brain is absolutely dependent upon his Senses.

He can only know what he has experienced through these five channels from the outer world to his brain.

When he comes to problems like the Reason for Creation, the Origin of Life, Man, Motion and Matter, he is beyond his depth. He can only speculate.

If it were a mere problem of odor, flavor, or sound, that could easily be cleared up, but here he is passing beyond the range and the reach of the Senses, consequently he must speculate.

It is a suggestive fact that no man becomes a philosopher until he attempts to know something that the Senses cannot interpret.

Hagel's philosophy of the non-existence of a personal God was formulated because he could not find God with his eyes, hear Him with his ears, nor contact Him with his other Senses.

He was driven by Sense Knowledge limitations to leave the world an orphan, without a Creator, without a Ruler, for he had denied God's existence.

The philosopher is always dangerous when he leaves

24

Sense Knowledge facts and begins to speculate.

Nowhere does Sense Knowledge seem so utterly helpless as when it begins to discuss God, spirit, and the beginning of things.

It cannot see man as a spirit being.

It cannot understand God as a spirit being.

Yet it recognizes that there is a hunger in man after God, call it a God hunger, that is ever searching, ever reaching out for something it cannot obtain through the Senses.

Because of this, we have Sense Knowledge religions beginning in idolatry and ending in philosophy and metaphysics. They all, like Hagel, deny the personality of God.

The reason is this: Their Senses cannot register sensation of spirit.

They can register the beat of the heart, and they know that life is functioning because their heart beats register regularly.

But they cannot see, they cannot hear, they cannot feel God.

They say that God has no personality.

They say that God is a great Universal Mind, without brains with which to function, for had He brains He would be a person.

They call this impersonal Mind, "Love," "Goodness," "Perfection."

You can see the absolute inability of Sense Knowledge to find God by itself.

You can see in the end how utterly desolate they become.

They form wonderful philosophical and metaphysical conceptions and teachings, and they have slogans and striking sayings and affirmations, but back of it there is no reality. They are the product of the knowledge of the Senses.

Their philosophy causes them to question the reality of Satan, of sin, of disease and temptation.

In order to solve the problem they boldly declare the non-existence of a personal God, of sin and judgment.

In doing this, they hope to get rid of their Sin Consciousness and of their Inferiority Complex.

This philosophy strikes at the very foundation of the Revelation of all that is given to us in Christ.

It is attempting to give the Peace and Joy and Rest of spirit that only Christ can give.

The reason they do this is because the church has failed to teach Paul's Revelation about Jesus' finished work.

Had there been given a clear exposition of the finished work of Christ, as unveiled in Paul's epistles, these new Sense Knowledge religions would never have gained the ascendancy over the church that they have today.

By denying sin, they attempt to get rid of the need of the substitutionary sacrifice of Jesus Christ.

By doing this, they deny the efficacy of His blood and of His vicarious suffering.

Let us briefly notice what God gives us in the Pauline Epistles. First, He gives us a complete Redemption. Satan is conquered, brought to naught. He is stripped of his authority and dominion.

Second, man is Redeemed from Satan's authority and by a New Birth is translated out of Satan's kingdom into the family of God.

Third, he is not only declared Righteous, but he is actually made "the Righteousness of God in Christ."

He has the position of a son in the family of God. He has authority over sickness and disease and the works of the adversary by the legal use of the Name of Jesus.

He has the actual Indwelling Presence of the Holy Spirit in his body, until now he can say, "Greater is He that is in me than he that is in the world."

Last, when he has finished his course here, he has a home in Heaven with his Father.

You can see that Sense Knowledge religions have given us but a theory, whereas God has given us reality.

They have a theory of God's non-existence, of the non-existence of a Judgment, of the non-existence of Satan, of the non-existence of sin, and of the non-existence of disease.

In this Sense Knowledge paradise, they hide themselves away from the realities that are unveiled to us in the Pauline Revelation.

Chapter Six

SEVEN MAJOR GUESSES

HE limitations of Sense Knowledge are very obvious.

There are certain barriers that cannot be crossed.

There are certain lands that cannot be explored by Sense Knowledge.

But a strange freak of Sense Knowledge is that when these boundaries of its ability are reached, it either turns philosophical, metaphysical, or speculative.

I want you to think of seven major guesses or speculations of Sense Knowledge.

First, Sense Knowledge does not know the origin of Creation or of Matter.

This lack of knowledge chagrins and humiliates Sense Knowledge and so it becomes bold in speculation.

The guesses in regard to Creation of the Universe and of Matter have filled volumes of books.

They do not know how Matter came into being, or when, or why.

Sense Knowledge has always denied a personal God; and because it has no God, it has no Creator, so Matter must create itself.

The second major guess is the Origin of Life.

This has been a painful subject to the speculative scientists.

The theories of the Origin of Life fill many volumes and text books, but no one with only Sense Knowledge knows where Life began.

28

Every guess, so far, has been laid aside for another, and today they are as far from absolute knowledge as they were when Darwin wrote the "Origin of Species."

Third, Sense Knowledge does not know the origin of Motion, or when the Stellar heavens first began their revolutions.

If they could discover the Origin of Life, they could discover the Origin of Motion.

Fourth, they have never discovered the origin of the government of the universe.

Here is a vast universe made up of constellations of stars and suns, each revolving in its realm and the entire mass revolving around a great center, and yet no one has been able to discover the Author and the Governor of these heavenly bodies.

Fifth, they never have been able to discover the Origin of man.

Their speculations and their theories have destroyed the faith of millions and wrecked the morals of two generations.

There is not one of them that is courageous enough to admit that Sense Knowledge cannot discover the Origin of man.

They do not know the Reason for man, nor man's destiny.

Man is here.

Sense Knowledge can only recognize what it sees and hears and feels.

Sixth, Sense Knowledge does not know the Origin of sin.

Some have even gone so far as to deny its existence; but its persistence, its evidence of organization, staggers the thinking man.

A denial does not destroy a fact.

Yet Sense Knowledge has no ability to tell where it came from, to point to a cure or a Redemption from its fatal effects.

Seventh, Sense Knowledge has no conception of the origin of death, the why of death, or what death is.

Sense Knowledge turns poet or becomes metaphysical in the presence of this unknown enemy that hounds us from the cradle to the faltering steps of old age.

Sense Knowledge may become lyrical in its presence, but it has no solution.

We have seen the limitations of Sense Knowledge.

These limitations are limitations that are sometimes vital to man's happiness.

Revelation Knowledge is needed to fill the gaps of Sense Knowledge.

Chapter Seven

GOD IS A SPIRIT

ESUS said to the woman of Samaria, "God is a spirit, and they that worship Him, must worship Him in spirit and in truth."

Man could not worship God in spirit unless he himself was a spirit. It has been hard for us to become spirit conscious, to realize that spiritual things are as real as material things.

We accept as a fact that God is a Spirit, but we never realized the implications tied up in that fact.

A spirit has personality, but not necessarily a physical body. Angels are spirits; demons are spirits.

We cannot visualize spirit beings.

We cannot see the spirit any more than we can see the mind.

We cannot see the force that lifts the tide.

We can see the results of it.

God is a Spirit, and, as a Spirit, He created material substance.

We know that He is not only a Spirit but He is a love Spirit.

We know that He is a faith Spirit.

We know that He spoke the Universe into being with a Word, and He rules the Universe by "the Word of His power."

We know that man is a spirit, that he belongs to God's class of being, that he is eternal, that he can live in a body. He is capable of partaking of the nature of God, and his highest development comes in fellowship with God.

We know that he was to fill a place in God's heart.

God wanted him, loved him and desired to impart His nature to him.

We know that spiritual things are as real as material things. We know since man is a spirit, the greatest forces in him are spiritual.

Love and hate, hope and faith are spiritual forces.

These forces are the forces that govern the world.

We know that when man fell in the garden, it was a fall from the presence of God, and from spiritual things to physical. When he left God's presence, he was utterly dependent upon his Five Senses for his sustenance and protection.

His body immediately became the source of all his knowledge.

This knowledge is obtained by contacts with physical things, or things that affect the Senses, such as the food that he tastes, the fragrance of the flowers that he smells, and the sounds that he hears.

He protected himself, and fed and clothed himself, through the aid of these Senses.

The knowledge that he has today has come to him through these five channels of contact with material things.

We know another fact: God cannot be found by the Senses or known by the Senses.

He, being a spirit, can only reveal Himself to spirits.

He can reveal Himself to our spirit through the Word.

For instance, we hear someone read the Word of God. The thing that is read is weighed and measured by our intellect, but in some way, which is inexplicable to reason, it affects our spirit. It answers a need.

By listening to the Word, it changes our spirit. This change is called the New Birth.

Before we were Born Again, our minds were in harmony with our unregenerate spirit.

Now that our spirit has been recreated, our minds become renewed by the Word.

Now the two, our spirit and our mind, are brought into harmony.

We get to know the Father as really in our spirit as we get to know physical things through our Senses.

Faith in the Father and in spiritual things becomes as strong and well defined as faith in natural things.

We know that we can approach our Father and meet Him; that He will hear our prayer as really as we know that the sun will shine.

We know that His Word will become absolutely true in our lives.

Spiritual things are as real as physical things.

Spiritual hunger and spiritual thirst cannot be satisfied with philosophy or metaphysics.

They may charm the intellect, but the hour will come when the spirit will speak out of its hunger.

One of the things that we have learned in praying for the sick is that people are sick in spirit as well as sick in body.

The physical sickness will leave when we can bring perfect healing to the spirit.

We have found that fear and doubt are spiritual diseases and their reactions upon the spirit are similar to the reactions of cancer and T. B. and other deadly diseases on the body.

We find that as soon as we can bring perfect assurance that the disease was laid on Christ, and the mind comes to agree with the spirit, healing is inevitable.

SOME FACTS ABOUT THE HUMAN SPIRIT

There can be scientists in the realm of the spirit as well as in the realm of the Senses.

It has always been hard for Sense Knowledge men to accept spiritual things.

They tell you they cannot believe in miracles, they're unscientific.

This is because they live in the realm of their physical bodies.

Sense Knowledge cannot find God and would not know God if it found Him.

Sense Knowledge doesn't know how creation came into being, doesn't know why it came into being.

It does not know the origin of life, light, motion, or of gravitation.

The spiritual scientist does not deal in theories.

He deals in facts.

The largest part of the progress of the Sense Knowledge scientist is in the realm of speculation.

Sometimes he is able to make his theories become realities.

The spiritual scientist has proven there is a God.

He knows it.

He has found that God, and knows Him.

He deals only with ascertained facts.

He has found the Reason for Creation.

He knows why Creation came into being.

He knows the Reason for man.

He has solved that difficult problem.

He has found the source of life.

He has found that man is a spirit being in the class with God, he is Eternal, he originally had an eternal body.

He was made to live with God eternally.

He has found that man is in God's class of being, so created that he can receive into his spirit the nature of God.

It is an unfortunate fact that the spirit of man has received so little attention.

We spend hundreds of millions of dollars training men's bodies.

We have spent uncounted millions in educating their minds. But no chair in any institution has ever been devoted to the culture and development of man's spirit.

Here are some facts about the human spirit:

It is the source of love. Love is not the child of reason, or of Sense Knowledge. Love is born in the spirit of man.

The thing that is often mistaken for love is mere sex attraction. That is a physical attraction that has to do with the Five Senses.

But love is the child of the human spirit.

It is the seat, the source of life. It is the part of man that receives Eternal Life from God.

It cannot be found in the human body, but it is there.

Originally the spirit dominated the physical body and dominated the avenues through which the mind received its knowledge.

In the beginning the human spirit governed the human reasoning faculties.

Wisdom comes from the Human spirit.

It is the fountain of wisdom.

Reason has nothing but knowledge.

Knowledge is something that the Senses gather from the material world around them and the forces in this material world.

The ability to use knowledge wisely is a spiritual thing.

It is wisdom that comes from the human spirit.

Faith is born of the human spirit.

Unbelief is largely the child of the Senses.

That is very suggestive.

You cannot develop faith through the reasoning faculties, no matter how much you try to do it.

Faith is born in the human spirit.

Fear and courage are both spiritual forces.

They come from the same source.

Joy and peace are not mental attributes.

They are spiritual.

The human spirit has given birth to the greatest forces in civilization.

Gal. 5:22 "The fruit of the spirit is love, joy, peace." That is the fruit of the recreated spirit, not the fruit of the Holy Spirit, because the Holy Spirit does not bear fruit only as He bears it through the branches of the vine, the body of Christ.

Chapter Eight

GOD'S ANSWER TO SPIRIT HUNGER

MAN'S spirit feels its orphaned condition.

Jesus came to answer this cry of the spirit, this cry for a Father, this cry for Redemption from the powers that surround it and hold it in bondage.

The four gospels are written in the realm of Sense Knowledge.

There is no inkling of the Revelation that God was to give to Paul in any of them.

They saw the miracles. They saw the man Jesus arrested. They saw Him tried in court.

They heard the sentence pronounced upon Him.

They saw Him go with the soldiers, bearing His Cross to the death hill—Golgotha.

They saw Him nailed to the cross.

They saw the cross lifted up and dropped into its socket.

They saw the blood dripping from the wounds in His hands and feet.

They heard Him cry, "My God, my God, why hast thou forsaken me?"

They could see the nails holding His trembling body on the tree.

They saw Him die.

But they could not see the tragedy in His soul.

They could not see His spirit made sin.

They could not see the spirit leave the body and go to the place of suffering under the dominion of the Black Prince.

They could not see Him as He suffered until the claims of Justice were met.

They could not see Him when He was justified, having paid the penalty of man's transgression.

They could not see Him when He became the First Born out of Death. This was the birth of His spirit out of spiritual death.

They could not see Him when He met the adversary, conquered him, and stripped him of his authority.

They could not see Him until He came back to his body and imparted Immortality to it, bursting the bars of death and standing before them absolute Master of Satan, death, and the grave.

He had to say, "Come, handle me, a spirit hath not flesh and bones," before their Senses could grasp the fact of His Resurrection.

He ate the fish and bread in their presence to prove that He had risen from the dead.

He appeared among them for forty days, then, from Mt. Olivet, He ascended, and an angel host convoyed Him to the throne of God where He sat down at the Father's right hand as our Mediator, Intercessor, Advocate, and Lord.

On the ground of this work, unseen by human eye, not felt by human Senses, but given to us in the Revelation to the Apostle Paul—on the ground of this, man's spirit can be Recreated, set free from the thraldom that has held him through the ages.

This remarkable thing is called a New Birth.

I know of no title that is so suggestive.

You accept Jesus Christ as your Savior, confess Him as your Lord; and God recreates you, imparts to your spirit His very nature.

Your spirit now is Made Alive in Christ.

You become a New Creation, created in Christ Jesus.

Now the benefits of it are imparted to you.

Now your spirit can fellowship God.

Now your spirit can enjoy something that your mind, the child of your Senses, cannot grasp.

We come to the next phase of this miracle thing.

Your mind, which had been dominated by the Senses, receiving all of its knowledge through the nerve centers, is being renewed through the Word so that it is coming into fellowship with your recreated spirit.

Your spirit is gaining the ascendancy over your thinking faculties.

Your Senses are taking their proper place.

You put the crown upon your spirit.

Your spirit becomes the master of your being.

Previously your physical body had been the master.

By this New Birth, your spirit comes into its own.

You are not living by Sense Knowledge, but you are living by the Word of God.

Jesus' Words, "Man shall not live by bread alone, but by every Word that proceedeth out of the mouth of God," are becoming a reality.

You say, "Thy Word is more precious than my necessary food."

You feast on the Word, you meditate on it until it becomes a part of your very being.

The most miraculous thing about it is that your intellect may not be fruitful when you read from some sections of the scripture, and yet, your spirit feeds upon it, and you become strong and vigorous in your spirit life as a result.

Chapter Nine

THE THREE WITNESSES

OR many years I have been bothered because I could not understand why people who had received their healing and had all the evidence of perfect deliverance should have the disease come back again, and then find it almost impossible to get deliverance.

I believe I have made the discovery.

Their faith was not in the Word of God, but in Sense evidence.

What do I mean by Sense Evidence? I mean the evidence of their sight, hearing and feeling.

They were like the sick folk that came to the Master. They had heard that He had healed some of their friends.

They said, "If I can get to Him, I will get my healing."

As they drew near they saw men healed. The blind were made to see; the deaf were made to hear.

They cried out for their share of the blessing and were healed.

Today there are many that come to us for healing because the Father has been gracious in healing many in our ministry.

Many have no time to be taught in the Word. They have no interest in the Word, all they are interested in is getting their deliverance.

We pray for them. They are instantly healed.

In a little while they come back again and say, "I can't understand it. That healing did not stand up. All the symptoms are back again."

Where was the difficulty?

It lay in this: They had no faith in the Word of God. They knew nothing about the Word as far as healing was concerned.

Their faith was in me, or in some other person, but not in the Word.

The Word declares, "By His stripes ye were healed."

Take this as an illustration. A gentleman came to me with a very bad knee. The doctors had told him that an amputation might be necessary.

He was instantly healed when I prayed for him.

Five or six days afterward, while he was walking on the street, that old pain returned.

He said, "This cannot be; I am healed by His stripes. In Jesus' Name, pain leave my knee." That man stood on the Word and the pain left, never to return.

The others stood on Sense Evidence, what they could see, what they could feel or hear.

They lost their healing because there was no "depth of soil," as Jesus put it in the parable of the sower.

In every case of healing there are three witnesses.

The Word.

The Word of God declares, "By His stripes ye were healed."

The Pain.

There is the witness of pain in the body, and that pain declares that it is not healed. The pain is severe and the sick person can hear nothing but pain.

The Sick One.

The sick one declares, "By His stripes I am healed, placing his witness or testimony along by the side of the Word of God. He refuses to take his testimony back.

He declares in the face of pain—in the face of Sense Evidence—that he is healed and he holds fast to his confession and God makes it good.

He is healed.

But often, when we open the Word and prove that "By His stripes they were healed," they say, "Yes, I can see that, but the pain is still here; the pain has not left my limb."

They have repudiated the Word of God. They have accepted the testimony of their Senses rather than the Word.

I can pray for them again and again, but I get no results because they witness against the Word of God.

You take another case. Here is a woman who is weak; she cannot walk.

I bring her the Word that, "The Lord is the strength of my life, of whom shall I be afraid?"

She says, "Yes, I see that scripture, but I cannot walk."

She repudiates the Word of God. The testimony of her lips joined with the testimony of her Senses disavows the Word of God, and she remains ill.

On the other hand, had she steadfastly maintained her testimony that the Word was true in the face of contrary Sense Evidence, healing would have been hers. But she rejected the Word because of the witness of her pain.

I discovered something else.

He says, "If thou shalt confess with thy mouth Jesus as Lord, and shall believe in thy heart that God raised Him from the dead thou shalt be saved" or "healed."

Many confess it with their lips, but deny it in their heart.

They say, "Yes, the Word of God is true." But in their heart they say, "It is not true in my case. He hasn't healed me. He healed others, but I am no better."

The confession of your lips has no value as long as your heart repudiates it.

There must be the testimony of your lips and the confirmation of the Word in your heart.

I am sure that the majority of people who have been prayed for and do not get their healing have no assurance in their hearts. They are desperate. Sense Knowledge has failed. They turn to God but have no real faith.

Healing is always in response to faith's testimony.

The pain may be fearful, but you have seen that "By His Stripes you are healed."

You know it as you know that two and two are four.

You are convinced in your innermost being that God has healed you. You look up and say, "Father, I thank thee."

You pay no attention to the pain. You ignore the symptoms because you know in the Father's mind you are healed.

The Word declares you are healed.

What the Word says is true.

You maintain your testimony in the face of evidence that is contrary to the Word, and God makes it real in your life.

Chapter Ten

WHAT THE WORD SAYS ABOUT SENSE KNOWLEDGE

AL. 1:11-12, "For I make known to you, brethren, as touching the gospel which was preached by me, that it is not after man. For neither did I receive it from man, nor was I taught it, but it came to me through Revelation of Jesus Christ."

What I found in Paul's epistles first awakened me to this subject.

I never understood his reference to the word "flesh" in Rom. 8:1-12, until I saw that word "flesh" means "Senses."

Take this as an illustration. "For they that are after the flesh, mind the things of the flesh; but they that are after the spirit, the things of the spirit."

Now read it this way. "For they that are after the Senses have the mind of the Senses, but they that are after the spirit have the mind of the spirit."

It is not speaking about the Holy Spirit. It is speaking about our spirit.

Seventh verse, "The mind of the flesh (that is the thinking that derives its evidences from the Senses) is enmity against God."

He does not mean the physical body as the physical body, but the physical body as holding the five channels through which knowledge comes to our intellect.

The body is the repository of the Five Senses through which all the knowledge of material things has come to our brain.

44

I Cor. 1:21, "For seeing that in the wisdom of God, the world through its wisdom knew not God, seeing the Jews ask for signs and the Greeks seek after Sense Knowledge."

This is illuminating. Here is the knowledge of God, or Revelation Knowledge, over against Sense Knowledge of the world.

It declares that this Sense Knowledge does not know God—cannot know God. This perfectly agrees with I Cor. 2:14, which reads, "Now the natural man receiveth not the things of the spirit of God; for they are foolishness unto him; and he cannot know them, because they are spiritually understood."

This is God's statement of fact.

Man has failed to get the knowledge of God, though he has given himself to study and searching through all the realms of nature.

The philosopher has always been reverenced in every age.

We little appreciate what the true philosopher is. He is really a searcher after God, because he has failed to find satisfaction in anything else.

He has never arrived at reality, the aim of all philosophers.

You cannot find reality anywhere outside of Jesus Christ.

The old scientists were all God seekers, but Job tells us they cannot find God by searching.

The scripture I just quoted tells us that Sense Knowledge cannot know the things of God.

Sense perception fails utterly when it comes to divine things.

Men who are not Born Again have no place in the pulpit,

45

as teachers of Sunday School classes, or as teachers in our theological institutions, because they have nothing in themselves but Sense Knowledge.

Col. 2:2-3, "That they may know the mystery of God, even Christ, in whom are all the treasures of wisdom and knowledge hidden."

This is where true Knowledge, true Wisdom heads up.

I Cor. 1:26, "Behold your calling, brethren, that not many wise after Sense Knowledge, not many mighty, not many noble, are called."

I Cor. 2:2 throws light upon Paul's idea of the ministry. "For I determined not to know anything among you, save Jesus Christ, and Him crucified."

Paul had had the advantages of all the scholarship of his age; with his unusual intellect he had gathered much knowledge. But he said, "When I came to you, I laid aside my knowledge, and gave you what I had in Christ.

"And my speech and my preaching were not in the persuasive words of Sense Knowledge, but in demonstration of the Spirit and of power; that your faith should not stand in the Sense Knowledge of men, but in the ability of God."

Read carefully the next few verses and you see a contrast of the two kinds of knowledge.

You can understand how Paul gave up Sense Knowledge for Revelation Knowledge.

He tells us in I Cor. 2:9, "Things which eye saw not, and ear heard not, and which entered not into the heart of man, whatsoever things God prepared for them that love Him."

It is not wisdom and knowledge that has come through the eye or the ear, but it has come through Revelation.

10th verse, "But unto us God revealed them through the Spirit. But the Spirit searcheth all things, yea, the deep things of God."

Sense Knowledge cannot penetrate here.

The superior Knowledge which has come through Revelation takes its place.

"But we received not the spirit of the world (or of this age) but the Spirit which is from God; that we might know the things that are freely given to us of God. Which things we speak, not in words of man's wisdom (or Sense Knowledge), but in words that the Spirit has given to us. For the natural man receiveth not the things of the Spirit of God: for they are not intelligible to him."

This is so suggestive.

How it challenges us.

Now we can understand why a ministry that is ruled by Sense Knowledge cannot build faith in the hearts of the congregation.

We can understand why Sense Knowledge does not believe in Revelation, does not believe in miracles, does not believe in the supernatural.

A man may be a child of God and yet never have his mind renewed. He still lives in the realm of Sense Perception. He cannot know the things of God.

Sense Knowledge has closed the doors against the teaching of the Holy Spirit and Revelation.

The only solution to this problem is the recognition of the Lordship of Jesus Christ, which really means the Lordship of the Word.

This Revelation is the mind of Christ that has been given

to us, that we might know our own Father-God.

Only as we recognize the Lordship of this Word does the light of the Spirit dawn upon us.

Discrediting evidence gained through the Senses is not an easy task.

The more we study this subject the more vital it becomes.

We are to cast down the world mind and all its Knowledge and accept the Revelation of God in its place.

You cannot build faith as long as Sense Knowledge sits upon the throne of your reason.

As long as you listen to the reasonings derived from the Senses you will never believe the Word, you will never walk by faith, you will never see the triumphs of faith in your life.

What Jesus said to Martha at the tomb of Lazarus fits this age in which we are living.

When Jesus said, "Roll ye away the stone," Martha said, "Lord, he has been in the tomb four days. His body decayeth."

Sense Knowledge held Martha.

Jesus said so tenderly to her, "Said I not unto thee, that, if thou believedst, thou shouldest see the glory of God." Martha saw the glory of God, but I question if she appreciated it.

Take this case as an illustration.

Here is a woman healed of cancer. It was a hideous thing. God wrought a miracle before the people, and Sense Knowledge folks said, "Well, it might not have been a cancer."

Another said, "Perhaps it was her time to get well anyway, just nature taking its course."

Sense Knowledge will not give God the credit.

The only thing to do with Sense Knowledge is "to cast it down" and let Revelation Knowledge, the Word of God, take its place.

One of the most vivid contrasts given to us in the Old Testament is found in Jer. 17:5-8.

"Cursed is the man that trusteth in man, that maketh flesh his arm, whose heart departeth from Jehovah."

Let us read it this way, "Cursed is the man that trusteth in Sense Knowledge and maketh Sense Knowledge his strength, whose heart has departed from Jehovah."

There you have the contrast.

One leads us invariably away from God to trust in what man has done, and the other leads us to trust in the Lord.

7th verse, "Blessed is the man that trusteth in Jehovah, whose trust Jehovah is."

Read these verses carefully and note the contrast of Sense Knowledge faith and Revelation faith.

Sense Knowledge faith is in what man is, and can do, and has done.

Revelation faith is in the Word of God, "That liveth and abideth."

Chapter Eleven

OUR SENSES AND THE WORD

THERE will always be a conflict between our Senses and the Word.

The Word demands that we walk by faith; the Senses demand that we walk by sight.

The Word demands absolute obedience. The Senses rise in rebellion against it.

The Senses have held sway so long that it is hard to yield their dominion to the Word.

Walking by faith is simply walking according to the Word.

It leads us out of the realm of the Senses into the realm of the spirit.

"For we look not at things that are seen, but things which are unseen.

Perhaps the most striking scripture in this connection is II Cor. 10:3-5, "For though we walk in the flesh we do not war according to the flesh: for the weapons of our warfare are not of the flesh, but mighty before God to the casting down of strongholds; casting down reasonings, and every high thing that exalts itself against the Word of God, and bringing every thought into captivity to the obedience of Christ."

To walk in the flesh is to walk according to the Senses.

Our walk is in the spirit and the weapons of our warfare are the weapons of the Word.

"The strongholds" are those created by Sense Knowledge where men defend themselves against the Word.

They are false reasonings.

They are denials of the supernatural, denials of the authority of the Word of God.

We are bringing every thought into captivity to the Lordship of the Word.

Vain reasonings and vain imaginings are the enemies of Faith. They exalt themselves against the Word of God.

It is amazing how the opinions of men have crippled the church—filled the hearts of the ministry with fear.

Now we are bringing every Sense Knowledge thought "into captivity to the obedience of Christ."

When we are tempted by our friends to resort to Sense Knowledge methods for deliverance, we turn resolutely to the Word and trust in the Lord with all our heart.

When we are tempted to borrow money to pay our bills, we turn to the Word that declares, "My God shall supply every need of yours."

When we are tempted by our weakness and lack of ability, we remember that, "I can do all things in Him who strengthens me."

When my body is weak and the tasks are heavy I remember, "Jehovah is the strength of my life, of whom shall I be afraid?"

When I lack wisdom, I remember, "He is my light and my salvation, whom shall I fear?"

You rest upon Sense Knowledge, and it often breaks.

Your rest is turned into misery. But when you rest upon the Word, it can never fail you.

Sense Knowledge is always crying "our lack, our need," and asking, "What are we going to do now? There is not a dollar left. How will we pay our bills?"

The Word declares: "Your Heavenly Father knoweth that ye have need of all these things."

I can hear Him whisper in the midst of the confusion of Sense Knowledge reasonings, "Hold fast the confession of your faith."

Our confession is always taking sides either for the Word or against it.

When we are sick, we hear the Word, "By His Stripes we are healed." Every time that we confess our weakness and our failure, confess that our wants have not been met, we are unconsciously taking sides against the Word.

When we say, "I am so weak I can't do this work," that is a confession of Satan's supremacy over us and his ability to thwart the will of the Father in our lives.

Most of the confessions that we hear today are confessions of lack, confessions of failure, confessions of Satanic supremacy in our lives.

Faith cries, "My God shall supply every need." "No Word from God is void of power."

The Word gains the mastery of the Senses.

If we look at our weakness and lack of money and say, "I don't know how I will succeed, or how I will pay my rent"; we have lost the battle.

If, on the other hand, we declare, "God is my supply and the strength of my life," and "Nay, in all these things I am more than a conqueror," we become victors.

Faith declares, "God is watching over His Word to perform it."

David said the most unique thing. "Thou preparest a table before me in the presence of mine enemies, my cup runneth over."

In the presence of failure, in the presence of weakness, in the presence of the witnesses that Sense Knowledge can bring to contradict the Word of God, I shout David's song of praise that "God has prepared a table for me in the presence of these Sense Knowledge enemies."

Chapter Twelve

WALKING BY THE SENSES YET SEEKING
REVELATION RESULTS

OST Christians have not yet learned to walk by faith. Their minds are still receiving directions for life through the avenues of the Senses.

To walk by Faith, we mean to walk by the Word of God.

To walk by the Senses is to walk by reason, yours or someone else's.

A woman came to me the other night asking me to pray for her child.

She said, "The doctors have done all they can. They say there is no hope."

I asked her why she didn't go to the Father first.

She said, "I thought about it, but I didn't know what to do so I called the doctor."

That is Sense Knowledge facing human limitations and crying out in fear for help from the unseen God.

She could trust in the doctor because she could see him; she could see the medicine, but she could not trust in the Word because she could not see God.

She could not hear His voice.

But when the doctor failed, she turned to God for help.

The amazing thing is the Grace and Love of the Father-God.

He instantly touched the child and brought deliverance.

Sense Knowledge had reached its limit.

The doctor knew all about the organs in the child's body.

He could visualize the inflammation that had laid hold on

54

that particular organ, and yet he had no means to allay the inflammation or to effect the cure.

But faith says, "God created the human body and so He is the logical healer."

Faith says that God laid that disease on Jesus. Jesus bore that disease, and so the child does not need to bear it.

So I lift up my heart to Him and say, "Thank you that the child is well, that the disease was laid on Jesus and the child does not need to bear it."

The child is well.

Sense Knowledge cannot understand it.

It ridicules it. It says, "It can't be," and yet there is in every man the God hungry spirit, the faith hungry spirit, and the spirit cries out against reason that has closed the doors against God, cries out against reason that sought man to do the work that only God has the right and the ability to do.

I venture to say this: Every man or woman that reads this book is conscious in his spirit that he is a spirit, that he needs God, that he needs faith, that he needs love that can come only from God.

RIGHT AND WRONG THINKING

Man has always sought independence of God.

A few years ago one man said when he considered the great achievements of chemistry, "We shall soon be independent of God."

He thought that through the avenues of chemistry and irrigation, they would be independent of God, but he had to have the sunlight, he had to have the wind. He had to have life that only God can give.

How little he appreciated it.

Sense Knowledge is ever seeking to push God off the throne, to usurp the place that only God can fill.

So it is in the spiritual life, Sense Knowledge seeks independence from God in spiritual things.

Men think they can get along without God, they can make their own way, they can plan their own future.

I said to one of these men recently, "What about heaven?"

He said, "If there is such a place as heaven, we are going to merit it by our deeds and our works."

Sense Knowledge would take the place of Jesus Christ as a Savior.

How much we are like Rom. 1:28 where they refused to have God in their knowledge.

We have reached that place in our educational systems.

We have thrown the Bible out of our Schools, our Colleges and our Universities.

It no longer holds a place.

Our teachers ridicule it.

In the business world they have invited the other god to take the place of Jesus Christ.

The business world is in a state of chaos because it thought it could get along without God.

We thought we could get along without God in our homes, and one out of every three homes go upon the rocks and our children are thrown upon the world without home influences.

How little we have realized that we are robbing ourselves, we are limiting ourselves, we are denying ourselves the rare privilege of having Him in our Schools, Colleges, Universities and in the business world and home.

How we have deceived ourselves. How we have robbed our nation of the influence of a living Christ in our national life.

Whenever a man thinks that Reason is safer than Revelation, that Reason is better than Revelation, he is stepping out of light into darkness.

When we turn down the lordship of Jesus Christ to accept the lordship of our own Reason, we make a blunder that has desolation as its conclusion.

Refusing to have Jesus Christ as the head of our home, as the head of our business, as a teacher in our Schools, is one of the saddest mistakes we have ever made.

Think how beautiful it is when we can say, "The Lord is my shepherd, I shall not want," when we say "The Lord is the strength of my life of whom shall I be afraid," when we can say, "My Lord is a present help in every time of need."

How beautiful it is when we can say to our children, "We are inviting Jesus and the Father to come and make their home with us."

The children see the parents reverently bow their heads over the food and thank the unseen One for it, and then they hear the parents pray for them before they go to school that they may be watched over, cared for, and they will be enabled to get their lessons.

It adds sanctity and beauty and safety that nothing else has ever been able to do.

Sense Knowledge that repudiates the Bible is really our worst enemy.

Chapter Thirteen

HOW TO RECEIVE ETERNAL LIFE

WE HAVE seen the great importance of receiving Eternal Life.

We have seen not only its great importance but its effect upon the human mind.

We know that it is more important than any other one thing to human happiness and the progress of the nation.

We know that the convulsions that are in the civil political, educational and financial world would all be quieted and smoothed out if the leaders of the nation would receive Eternal Life.

It would solve every problem.

It is a strangely interesting fact that you could not find a man and woman that had received Eternal Life and were walking in fellowship with the Father that ever went to the divorce court.

People who have received Eternal Life have received the nature of God, and they hold such a sacred conception of marriage, home, and children that a divorce court is a thing of abhorrence.

People who have recognized the Lordship of Jesus find it makes life a beautiful, successful enterprise.

How can one receive Eternal Life?

It is very simple. Let us begin with Is. 53:6. "All we like sheep have gone astray; we have turned every one to his own way; and the Lord hath laid upon Him the iniquity of us all."

Notice that first phrase, "All we like sheep have gone

astray." The sin problem here is thrown upon the screen.

We have turned everyone to his own way, that is the way of self gratification, the way of the Senses.

Then: "God laid on Him (Jesus) the iniquity of us all," and He puts it away.

Jn. 1:12, "As many as received Him, to them gave He the right to become children of God, even to them that believe on His name."

Here is the Savior that God provided.

He says, "As many as received Him" as their Savior, God gave the legal right to sonship and to sonship privileges and blessings.

Everyone who receives Him shall receive Eternal Life.

What are the conditions of receiving Him?

Rom. 10:9-11 is God's answer. "That if thou shalt confess with thy mouth Jesus as Lord, and believe in thy heart that God raised Him from the dead, thou shalt be saved. For with the heart man believeth unto Righteousness; and with his mouth he makes confession of his salvation. And whosoever believeth on Him shall not be put to shame."

Let us go back and look at it carefully.

"That if thou shalt confess with thy mouth Jesus as Lord, and believe in thy heart that God raised Him from the dead."

We will begin with the second statement. You believe, as far as you know, that Jesus was raised from the dead.

You believe He died for your sins according to scripture, and the third day He was raised for your justification.

Now you confess Him as your Lord.

That is the solution of the problem from your end of the issue.

You confess His Lordship over you. That means a real turning away from everything else; that means a real repentance, if you please, for the instant you crown Jesus as Lord you strip the crown from self and Satan and put it upon Jesus Christ as the Master and Ruler.

"With the heart man believeth that Jesus is his Righteousness, and with his lips he confesses that He is Lord."

What has this given you?

Jn. 6:47, "He that believeth hath Eternal Life."

You believe. You have Eternal Life.

I Jn. 5:13, "These things have I written unto you that ye may know that ye have Eternal Life, even to you that believeth on His Name."

You have believed on His Name. You have accepted Him as your Savior, you have confessed Him as your Lord and now God takes you to be His child, and you are in His family.

Here are some additional facts that are vital to every one of us.

II Cor. 5:17-18, "Wherefore if any man is in Christ, he is a New Creation: the old things are passed away; behold they are become new. But all these things are of God, who has reconciled us unto Himself through Christ."

In this scripture you see that you who have accepted Jesus Christ are a New Creation.

Eph. 2:10, "For we are His workmanship, created in Christ Jesus."

You are reconciled to the Father.

For, "Him who knew no sin became sin that you might become, by this New Birth, by receiving Eternal Life, the Righteousness of God in Christ."

Now you have a right to go into the Father's presence just as Jesus does.

You have as good a standing as Jesus, because Jesus is now your standing.

He vouches for you.

There is, therefore, now no condemnation to you, because you are in Christ Jesus.

What does all this mean?

It means exactly what it says:

You are to act just as though it were true, because it is true.

You are to recognize its utter truthfulness, for it is all of God.

You are in His family. Take your place.

Now you are an heir of God, a joint heir with Christ. Now act it.

God now is the strength of your life.

You can do all things in Christ who is your enabling power, your ability.

You have received the very ability of God.

You have received the very strength of God.

You have received the very life of God.

The Love Law that Jesus gave is now the Law that is to govern your life.

"By this shall all men know that ye are my disciples, if ye have love one for another."

You have that love.

Now you must go and tell the story.

It is your business now to become a witness.

You are to tell the world.

Chapter Fourteen

SUMMARY OF REVELATION

OU have seen the utter failure of Sense Knowledge to grasp the significance of Revelation Knowledge. Now let me show you what Revelation Knowledge can mean to a man.

OUR REDEMPTION

God has done all that He could do in our Redemption. He gave His only begotten Son as a Substitute for our sins.

His finished work meets every need of man. He perfectly satisfied the claims of the Supreme Court of the universe against outlawed man.

When He planned our Redemption it covered every need. He knew what was required. He furnished a Redemption that utterly met the need of every man.

He has provided a perfect Redemption for Spirit, Soul and Body.

Since the Son has done that work for Him, He now stands ready to make good every promise in order to meet our faith for every need.

He has provided a perfect Righteousness for us, so that we may stand in His presence as though Adam had never sinned.

He not only Justified His own right to create man in the face of the fact that He knew man would fall, but He has gone beyond that in making it possible for every disease to be healed, every weakness turned to strength, all power of Satan nullified and to stand in His presence a righteous perfect being, an absolute New Creation created in Christ

Jesus.

THE INCARNATE ONE'S WORK

He became Incarnate, took upon Himself our limitations as a man, lived among us, and then permitted Himself, who knew no sin, to be made sin for us.

He became sick with our sicknesses; He became weak with our weaknesses.

He was an outcast and became a part of all we were, becoming Identified with all our weaknesses, sicknesses and diseases. Then He bore our sins and diseases away and suffered until every need of man was fully met.

Then God justified Him, because He had met the demands of the human race in His sufferings.

After being Justified He was made alive in Spirit. Then He met the Adversary, conquered him, stripped him of his authority and dominion, and arose from the dead.

Then He carried His blood into the heavenly Holy of Holies, poured it out before the Father on the mercy seat, and made an Eternal Redemption for us. All that Jesus did, He did for us.

His work is absolutely perfect. On the ground of that work any man can stand right with God; any man can be healed of all his diseases. Satan's dominion over the New Creation is utterly broken.

To Jesus was given the Authority that the first Adam forfeited, and with that restoration of Authority, there was given Him added dominion and power, because of what He had done for the salvation of the human race; that authority and dominion has been given to us in the legal use of His Name.

WORK OF THE HOLY SPIRIT

We know it was the Holy Spirit who raised Jesus from the dead.

We know that the Spirit has done all that was expected of Him to do, and that He stands ready now to make good in every one of our lives all that God wrought for us in Christ, to pour the very life and nature of the Father God into our mortal bodies and actually swallow them up in life.

"For it is God who worketh in you both to will and to work, for His good pleasure." Phil. 2:13. "Greater is He that is in you than He that is in the world." I Jn. 4:4.

The Spirit Himself will guide us into all truth. Jesus has done His part; the Holy Spirit has done His part. All three are ready now to meet every demand of yours.

They stand ready to meet your faith, whatever that faith may take. But they stand helpless and the work they have done for us is utterly of no avail unless we take what belongs to us.

BELIEVING IS TAKING

I have told you that "believing" is a verb, an action word, so all you need to do is to take what He has offered you.

First, it is accepting your salvation, eternal life, new birth and union with God; next, it is taking the great mighty Holy Spirit as your indweller, your guide and teacher, your healer and your overcomer; then, it is taking your perfect deliverance from the enemy for your Spirit, Soul and Body.

It is taking a perfect healing for your spirit, healing of the old wounds and diseases of unbelief, doubts and fears.

Now as He stands complete before the Father, you stand complete in Him before the Father.

64

There is therefore now no condemnation for you, because you are in Christ Jesus.

USE YOUR AUTHORITY

The old law of sin and disease in your body has been condemned, and you order it out in Jesus' Name.

Now you see yourself perfectly healed in your spirit. You know that all God has done for you becomes available, actually effecting a perfect healing and restoration. You have an absolute deliverance and healing of your mind, and it becomes effective now. You have perfect healing of your body.

You see, all that was wrought for you, all that belongs to you. You move up, and as you believe, you possess your perfect emancipation from disease, sickness and pain. It matters not whether it be tuberculosis, cancer, arthritis, ulcers or tumors.

Regardless of its nature, that disease was fastened in your spirit, in your mind, and finally it is showing its deadly power in your physical body.

You know that Jesus bore it.

You know that Jesus put it away, and you believe it is put away now.

You know that it no more belongs on your body, spirit, and soul than it does upon the spirit, soul and body of Jesus Christ.

You are a member of His body, and now you know that it has no place there.

Your believing His gracious Word drives it out of your system and you stand clean, healthy, and complete in Him.

Believing takes possession, enters in and becomes a possessor of the healing.

BELIEVING AND SUGGESTION

Suggestion is purely a human thing. You say mentally a thing is true, or I say it to you, and I keep saying it over until you receive my suggestion and act upon it.

That is not Christianity, that is Psychology.

That is not faith in Christ. That is faith in yourself; that is faith in your own mind. You believe that your mind has in it a God element that can drive disease out and drive success and health in.

But your faith is in yourself, because there is no God to the man that believes in suggestion. He has destroyed God utterly out of the firmament, and mentally he has taken God's place. He uses all the terms that we use, but he gives new meanings to them.

When he says "God" he means his higher self. When I say "God" I mean the Creator of the universe; there is no self mixed in it.

When I believe, I act upon the Word of God. When he believes he acts upon something to which his own mind has given birth. I act upon the Word of the Living God who raised Jesus from the dead and put disease and sickness away.

All that I am saying has been said in other chapters of this book, but this new angle may help you to grasp your privileges in Christ.

HOW SPIRITUAL WEAKNESS COMES

Spiritual weakness in the believer comes from the sense of his guilt, sin or unworthiness that continually confronts him. Whenever he attempts to pray, his unworthiness leaps into being and stands between him and the Father.

Faith loses its power, and the faculty through which believing functions becomes paralyzed. He can do nothing but stand passive and helpless in the presence of his sin-consciousness.

Now we know that God has put sin away. We know that we are New Creations created in Christ Jesus.

We know that God is the author of that New Creation, that what God has made clean we have no right to call unclean, and what God has justified we have no right to condemn.

We know another fact that we have been redeemed out of the hand of the enemy, translated out of the kingdom of darkness into the kingdom of the Son of His love, and that as redeemed men and women "There is therefore now no condemnation to us that are in Christ Jesus." We stand before the Father Redeemed, absolutely justified, or declared Righteous. That declaration has come from the very throne of God.

If God has Justified us and declared us righteous, who has a right to condemn us? Surely Jesus will not do it, because it was Jesus that died for us and now lives for us.

SATAN, THE ACCUSER

The only being that can lay a charge against us is the Devil, and God will not listen to him. We listen to the Devil's lie and believe it. Then we become impotent, and all that God has done in Christ is utterly of no avail as far as we are concerned.

If on the other hand we believe the Word, that we are justified, that we are righteous NOW, Satan loses his dominion over us.

Someone asked me yesterday, "Are we poor weak sinful creatures now, we who have been born again, we who are new creations?" I answered, "No, never."

Every time you think of yourself in that capacity, you annul everything that God has done for you, and you declare that the finished work of Christ is a failure. "What God has cleansed, make not thou common (or unclean)." Acts 10:15.

If God has declared us righteous, no one can condemn us. Everything belonging to your sin-life stopped being the moment you were born again. Everything that was offensive to the Father was destroyed, never to come back again.

You are just like a new-born babe without a single thing that condemns, utterly justified, and utterly declared righteous by God. As you stand before the Father, you are complete in Him who is the head of all principalities and powers.

COMPLETE IN HIM

I wonder if you have grasped the significance of that scripture in Col. 2:9, 10, that you are complete in Him "who is the head of all principality and power." God has put beneath His feet all authority, all power, all dominion and all orders of Satanic power. Eph. 1:19-23.

You in Christ stand absolutely complete, head over it all, in fellowship with the Father. As He is, so are you now, because you and He are utterly one, perfectly identified. As

68

He was redeemed out of Satan's dominion of death, you have been redeemed out of Satan's dominion.

As He is in perfect fellowship, you are in perfect fellowship. As He was declared righteous by the Supreme Court of the universe, you have been declared righteous.

For you to think you are weak, unworthy, unclean and unfit, is to slap the Lord in the face, and say, "God, my feeling, my own mind, and the theology of my church are truer, better than your Word."

All that Jesus is, He is for you. It is He who vouches for you. It is He who is your surety before the throne.

When you took Him as your Savior, you passed out of the realm of darkness, death, sin, and Satan's dominion into the realm of light and life as a member of the body of Christ. Jesus is the vine and you are a branch. You are a part of His very self; you could not be nearer the Father if you were Jesus Himself.

IDENTIFIED WITH HIM

You are a member of His Body; you are utterly identified with Him in the mind of the Father.

As Jesus was healed of all our diseases which He bore for us when He arose from the dead, so the moment that you were born into the family of God and became a new creation, disease and sickness lost their dominion over you.

Disease and sickness have no more right to reign in your body than they have a right to reign in the body of Jesus at the right hand of the Father, who as your Substitute once was made sick with your diseases, but now is healed and justified.

In the mind of the Father you were cleansed of all disease and sickness through your substitute.

What should you do in the face of this fact?

You say, "Yes, that is absolutely true, I am what the Lord says I am." That would be faith acting; that would be believing your way into the very heart of the thing. You believe what God says is true, and when you believe it is true, it becomes a reality to you. You act upon it.

Now grasp this: He was what you were. When He went on that cross, He took you over, took your sin, and became as you were.

You were weak; He became weak. You were sin; He became sin. You were under judgment; He went under judgment. You were sick; He took your sicknesses over.

He bore them away; You and your sicknesses and sins He carried with Him down into the dark regions.

Then He put it off from Himself. The Word says, "Having put off from Himself the principalities and the powers, He made a show of them openly, triumphing over them in it." Col. 2:15.

When He put off the principalities and powers He put off your sickness and diseases and your sins. He took them and you upon Himself when He hung upon the cross. Now He puts them all off and puts them all away.

All that He is you are right now. As He was made righteous when He put sin away, you were made righteous in Him.

"Him who knew no sin He made to be sin on our behalf; that we might become the righteousness of God.

You refuse to allow the law of sin to work in your body.

70

The law of sin is disease and sickness. That law has been condemned.

The Supreme Court of the universe has passed upon it. It has no standing now. Don't you permit it to lord itself over you. You refuse to be lorded over by disease and sickness.

Remember now that sin shall not lord it over you any longer, for you have been set free in Christ Jesus. Disease shall not lord it over you. Disease shall not say, "I am master of your body, stomach, bowels, heart, lungs or bronchial tubes." You refuse to allow any disease to hold any dominion over your body in any way.

"THE TRUTH SHALL MAKE YOU FREE"

You are free, made free by Christ Jesus who is the Lord of disease and sickness.

Fear shall no longer lord it over you. You are a free woman, a free man. You have been delivered from the bondage of fear.

Satan, the author of fear, has been defeated and conquered, and you reign in Christ over him. Satan shall no longer lord it over you, for you have learned "in whatsoever state you are, therein to be independent of circumstances.

You can do all things in Christ, He gives you the ability to put them through. People shall no longer dominate and rule you. You stand absolutely free in Christ.

He is your Lord, and He is the only one to whom you owe allegiance. Jesus alone is your Lord, and they shall not have dominion over you any longer.

Stand fast therefore in the liberty wherein Christ has made you free, and rejoice in your emancipation from sin, sickness and disease through Jesus Christ your Lord.

CONCLUSION

This field has been new to most of us, but it solves some of the most difficult problems that confront the university student.

It shows why the man who has never yet yielded to the Lordship of Jesus Christ cannot understand spiritual things.

It shows on the other hand, how the whole scheme of Creation, of Life and man's Redemption is an open book to the man who crowns Jesus the Lord of his life and accepts this Revelation Knowledge as coming from God.

Life becomes big, and rich, and wonderful, as we clasp hands with the Unseen.

The heart finds its haven when Jesus Christ sits upon its throne.

We have found that Sense Knowledge can never find God, can never know Him; but there stands by the side of everyone, a Guide to lead him into the new kind of Knowledge, the new kind of Life, to lead him out of failure and weakness and heart hunger, into the banqueting hall of Love.